Magic in a black box: Why Roku is Popular

Tips, Tricks and Hacks

Disclaimer and Terms of Use:

Effort has been made to ensure that the information in this book is accurate and complete, however, the author and the publisher do not warrant the accuracy of the information, text and graphics contained within the book due to the rapidly changing nature of science, research, known and unknown facts and internet. The Author and the publisher do not hold any responsibility for errors, omissions or contrary interpretation of the subject matter herein. This book is presented solely for motivational and informational purposes only.

Table of Contents

Introduction

It's a black box and yet, it is more than a black box that allows homeowners to stream content. Why are homeowners switching from satellite to these streaming players? One of the reasons Roku is popular is there are three different versions of the device and it has far more apps than other popular streaming devices including: Netflix and Hulu. It is as popular as YouTube, HBO's Go, Vudu, Showtime Anytime, and Amazon Instant. Its interface is simple and this makes it instantly a favorite because users do not have to struggle to learn how to use it and can watch their favorite TV channels, movies, and music without paying hefty monthly fees. The advantage Roku gives to its users is they can access some name-brand services, such as "Crackle" to find what they want. Since Roku is not owned by a major brand, this serves as an advantage. The company doesn't give its users the pressure of needing to pay for a monthly service, nor does it need to offer incentives to users who use their platform over other competitors.

Roku is reasonably priced. It can cost between $40-$99 and these options are for everyone, especially for those who do not want to sign up for an expensive multi-year contract with a cable company. At first glance, these black boxes do not seem interesting until you realize you can do much, much more than watch Netflix. Who knew a Roku would allow you to watch television shows that are not on the air any longer, unless you have cable? But, it also allows you to access social media sites without using a computer or a Smartphone. If you own a Roku, you know your device isn't only a pretty, black box which allows you to watch television shows, it also allows you to listen to your favorite radio stations. This is only one of the many functions that are available to Roku owners.

A media device that works across multiple platforms

Roku is a black box that works well with Apple devices, but it can be used with Internet Explorer and Gmail. This black box works with so many different developers, but it also changes how we view a television. Televisions are not solely for viewing your favorite TV shows, but also for checking voicemail, and texting. Roku allows people to see a television's other capabilities when boosted by technology. It allows us a mode of communication and the capability to store our purchase information on a Roku. This report will explore all the things that you can do with a Roku (such as turn it into a DVR), how to reach secret screens for your Roku on your television, fix some of the bugs that could bother you and how to get music, movies and more, without paying a dime!

Computer screen with the mouse of downloaded content

Tip 1 - Install YouTube on your Roku

If you want to watch any funny videos, downloading YouTube is a good idea. This channel is free, and it can be added to a Roku player if it is added as a private channel. However, it will work for Roku users who have Roku 2 or Roku 3. It may not work for users who only have a Roku 1, the very first model of this streaming platform. Do not forget to enter a special code of B8VVK, so you can get YouTube on your device. If you need more help trying to get this channel on your machine, you can always visit the Roku.com website.

Look for private channels

Tip 2 - Looking for Private Channels

Do not think that YouTube is the only private channel that is worth watching or is the only one that is available to download. There are many private channels that users can find through their Roku that may not fit the usual content offered by Roku. They are considered experimental, but this does not mean you cannot watch them. For example, some companies offer adult entertainment that Roku users must pay extra to access. There is one channel that offers access to all podcasts that are on iTunes. Another channel may display a screensaver that has your Twitter account. Why not tweet to your friends via your Roku? While some of the channels may not be monitored, others are, such as the Roku Youth Group, available on Roku-channels.com. Roku has two lists of channels for users. Roku has a list of featured channels that are suggested channels at their website, Roku.com. There is also a list of channels available in the Roku channel store.

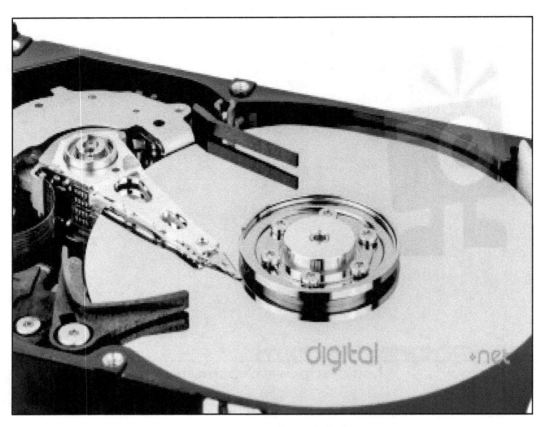

Computer hard drive

Tip 3 - Play content from your computer's hard drive

The newer Roku 3 allow users to access USB ports. By having access, users can play items off their flash or hard drives. Roku also has a private USB channel that users can access to find content if they enter code KGULU. If users wish, they can also upload their own USB content or flash content to a private channel. There have been mixed reviews about the quality of using this USB channel. This, however, could be before Roku offered an officially supported USB port for users to enjoy content from desktop or laptop's hard drives.

Keep in mind there may be more than one USB channel and those who enjoy this platform have more content to search and enjoy. With the ability to provide more than 1,800 on the Roku 3 alone, it is not surprising that new users of the Roku may not be familiar with all that the machine can offer its Roku family. While the company still makes a Roku 1 and Roku 2, the Roku 3 is the only one of the three that provides this advanced technology and this fun, extra feature. At $99, the Roku 3 is as affordable as its competitors and offers extras, such as the USB port, that other companies do not include in their streaming device designs.

Watching 'live' TV

Tip 4 - Watch live television on any Roku device

All a user must do before watching an episode of 'Cold Case' is to install the UStream channel. Did you know that you may add this to your machine as a private channel? Using channel code IN4DN, users have access to local events on the local NBC channel. What do you like to watch most? From sporting events to live concerts, local events may be watched on a Roku. Watchers also may not want to forget there are also a number of other streaming channels of local events for them to peruse.

Woman enjoying music on a local channel

Tip 5 - Play local channels that allow you to stream music, local channels, and videos

Take advantage of those local channels. They are another way Roku users can be informed of what is happening locally, via local channels, such as Roksbox. This app utilizes the web server on a computer and allows you to play local media. It is easy to operate, after all, you only have to open your system preferences, go to share and enable web sharing. Use channel code P1KWQ to install a private Roksbox channel on your Roku.

Converting XDIV Files

Trick 6 - Convert your videos so you can play them all using Handbrake

If you want to play every video you own, you may want to download Handbrake. It converts videos of almost every format and works in Mac, Windows, and Linux. The best news (if you are on a tight budget) is that it is free. Most Rokus (2 and 3, with the possible exception of the older Roku model 1's) will play only MP and MOV files. A Roku won't play DivX , xdiv, and other files. However, using the Handbrake app will help you convert files and Roku.com has listed the settings needed to use Handbrake successfully.

Trick 7 - Send photos to your family on your Roku

Give your family a Roku and you both can exchange photos, Roku to Roku. It also makes it handy to store your photos. What if you need to update photos? Did you know that you can use Roku simultaneously with a media sharing app, such as Dropbox? Dropbox makes it easy to send photos to your family's email box. As long as you both have Roksbox and Dropbox, new photos can be placed in Dropbox and be automatically available for sharing on a Roku. Sharing new photos is easier and you do not have to keep making new albums to place the most recent photos.

Trick 8 - Check your Google Voice

Did you know that you can do this via your Roku? Enter the channel code NXFBW and make certain that you have Google installed on the Roku. Log into your Google Voice account, and check it without having to pick up your phone. A developer was the one who thought of this trick. However, some users have reported it does not work perfectly for them. Google Voice is handy for users who are able to use it with their Rokus because the program allows users to browse inboxes, voicemails and SMS messages, play voice messages, and send SMS messages to participants who you are conversing. It also allows to initiate calls with any telephone numbers that you are not currently having conversations with participants and send SMS messages to them. If you use Google Voice quite a bit, having this app can be a time-saver and allow you not to waste value phone minutes checking your messages on Google Voice.

Trick 9 - How to make the sound work when using a headphones with a Roku 3

The Roku 3 has a jack for headphones. For those who are disabled or need to be able to listen to their television without disturbing roommates, this feature can be handy. However, some Roku users have reported the television speakers shut off when the headphones were plugged in. There is a way to bypass this, though. Pressing the Roku remote volume buttons in this order can allow the volume to return and you can also use the headphones: Up, up, down, down, up,up,up, down, down, down. You will be able to control the volume without the speakers shutting off, if you use this trick.

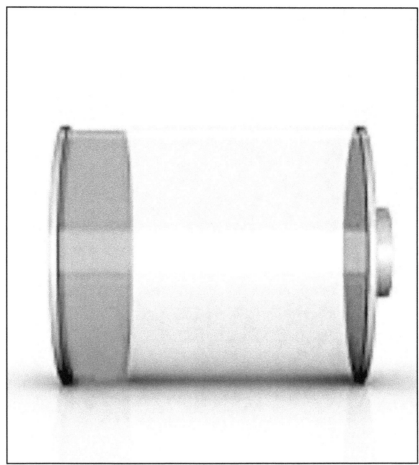

Making batteries in Roku remotes last

Tip 10 - Invest in rechargeable batteries for the Roku remotes

You may save yourself heartache and also the expense of having to run to the store so often for triple A batteries. While the Roku is handy and allows users to watch local channels, have access to Pandora, and Crackle, Netflix, Blockbuster and other channels, it can use up a great deal of energy. That energy can come in the form of draining the life of the new batteries that you place in a Roku remote. What is the advantage to having rechargeable batteries. These batteries will retain their battery life longer and you won't have to buy batteries as often. If you are concerned about your Roku quickly draining the life of your batteries, you can remove the batteries when you are not using your Roku device and put them in again when you want to watch your favorite movies or TV shows. Unplug headphones that are not being used as well, these may drain your Roku's batteries if not unplugged in a timely manner.

Freezing screen

Tip 11 - How to fix a Roku that causes a TV screen to freeze

Though the errors with refreezing (?) that seemed to affect Roku 2 seemed prevalent and Roku 2 systems were resetting, Roku 3 never is affected. Roku 3 never needs rebooting. How can customers who have a Roku 2 watch their favorite shows, without resetting every few minutes? One Roku user suggests rebooting a Roku from the remote, using the following sequence. Press the 'Home' button five times, then press the up arrow once, the rewind buttons twice and the fast forward button twice. Another way to help with a freezing screen is also to pop the batteries out of the remote when the Roku does freeze and reset the device.

Finding codes to find free Roku channels

Tip 12 - Find all the best TV channels that you can watch for free, Easily

Go to Streamfree.tv to find a listing of all the best television channels. This website does more than list the best Roku channels that users can watch, it also offers all the codes that Roku users should enter in order to download these private channels onto their Roku machines. If users want to watch older shows, download YouTube. Older shows, such as the 1960s, "Whose Line Is It, Anyway?" is available to watch. Users only need to download the YouTube channel onto their Roku, If Roku owners do not mind paying for a channel, there are more than 1,800 channels that users have access to. Some channels, such as Hulu, offer some free movies and shows, However, premium shows cost $9 a month. Some Roku channels may be downloaded for free, but users have to pay a fee to watch. Others may require Roku users to pay before downloading. In any case, Roku owners can find exactly what they want.

Use Roku in a hotel room

Trick 13 - Clone the Mac address on your Roku and use in-room at a hotel

Your Roku doesn't have an IP address because it cannot connect to the Internet, or does it? Did you know that you can bring your Roku into a hotel room? You can hook your Roku 3 up to your hotel TV. Here is how you manage such a complicated task. This trick will even work with older Roku models. Go to settings, network, and Roku settings in order to find out an IP address for your device. Power down and off your Roku and clone your IP address. For those who have a Mac and are running Windows, here is how to watch TV on your TV. On your computer, go to Terminal. At the command line, type in: ifconfig en1. It should give you an enter address, which may look similar to this: enter:68:a8:ee:ee:ee:fa. Write down your computer's Mac address. Finally, type in this command: sudo config, the address on your Roku model, (ie: en1) enter Roku-Mac Address.

shutterstock · 10739907756

No worries if you don't have a remote

Tip 14 - Control your Roku with your phone

You can use the Roku app on a Smartphone to control your Roku remotely. It also allows you to show photos from your phone and you can stream music from your phone, directly onto a Roku 3. You can also use the remote app on your phone to access the headphones feature and stream almost seemingly without being directly in front of your Roku device or the television. It is easy to pick up your Roku box and leave the house without your Roku remote. However, what if you don't discover your mistake until you are thousands of miles from home, with a Roku 3 player and no remote? If you forget to bring a the Roku remote and you have an Android phone, you can always download the Roku remote app directly from the Google Play Store onto your phone. Then, use your phone like a television remote.

Unlock developer mode on your Roku

Tip 15 - Modify apps to your liking by using developer mode

If you want to be able to override standard controls on apps and be able to modify them to your liking, it is possible to do that by clicking the following button sequence on your remote while you are on the home screen: home, home, home, up, up, right, left, right, left, right. Then, you will see a screen that ask if you want to enable an Installer, so that you can test your own apps. It is also give you an IP address at the bottom of the screen. You will need to record both your username and also your IP address. This IP address will be what you put into your computer when you are on the same network as your Roku. However, you must have your computer and Roku on the same network to be able to enter developer mode on your Roku. No worries about security because you will need to setup a password after you enable the installer by returning to the home screen and repeating the button sequencing on your remote again. After you set up a password, feed the IP address into your computer and you can download and modify whatever apps you wish.

Record your favorite shows

Trick 16 - Turn your Roku into a DVR

In order to watch TV using your Roku and turn it into a DVR essentially, you do need a USB stick that is plugged into your television. You also need to get a private channel through the Nowhere TV DVR. If you are on your Roku, you can add it to your Roku device. How does this work? The Nowhere TV DVR channel is able to convert live TV signals into shows that you can treat as a DVR program, pausing and starting when you wish. It will also let you make recordings that you can store to your Roku by using the Nowhere TV DVR channel. The quality may not be as great as a TiVO, but it is much cheaper than paying a large monthly fee. It may stutter a little, but it is a great way to record programming using a Roku box. Plus, you don't have to pay any expensive fees.

Optimize a home network on a Roku 2

Tip 17 - Optimize your home network if you have a Roku 2

This option will only work with a Roku 2 and not the newest because the Roku 3s use Wi-Fi. If your Roku 2 starts buffering and buffering, it may be the fact that the walls aren't letting the Wi-Fi signal through. When using a Roku 2, it is possible to use an Ethernet connection for your device. This will also allow you to get the best signal. Be aware though, it only works if you have a Roku 2 XS. The Roku XD, HD, LT and newer Roku 3 do not have the Ethernet port, but use Wi-Fi. If you still are not getting a good signal, move your Ethernet box closer to the living room or upgrade your Roku settings.

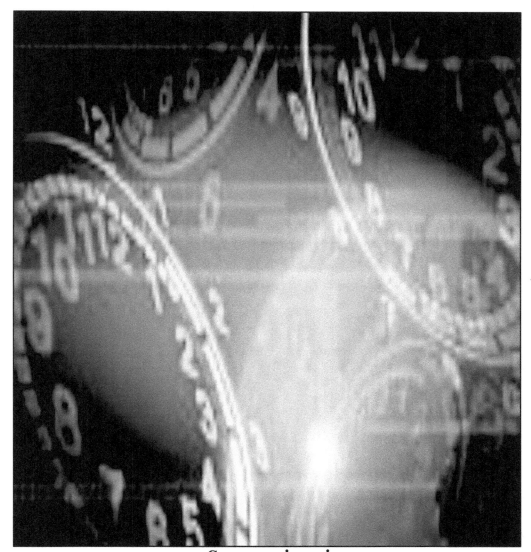

Screen mirroring

Tip 18 - Try Screen Mirroring in Beta for Windows and Android

While owning a Roku is wonderful, many of the apps for the program will not function on their own and users have to have additional equipment to make their Roku work like a DVR or to record some television programs. However, this problem may be solved with the new Screen Mirroring Beta. By using this on a phone that is Android capable or has Windows 8 capabilities, it is easy to install apps and make them work without special equipment. Once you turn on the mirroring on your phone, you can also see the same image on your Roku. This makes it easy to display what you are seeing directly onto your television. This trick only works with the newest Roku, Roku 3 model 4200 and the streaming stick 35000. At this time, it is not available to Apple devices. These may be options for the future.

Add a Plex server and app to your Roku

Tip 19 - Add Plex to your Roku

If you have a great deal of video content on your computer, you may want to consider using a Plex Media Server. By using the media server, a media manager will allow you to add videos that you can share with your Roku device. However, the Plex app is also available on the Roku interface, so finding this app is easy. Do keep in mind Plex videos may not be downloaded in a format that can be readily played by your Roku player. Roku users may also need Handbrake in order to successfully view Plex video content. Plex also gives Roku users access to programming that may not be available elsewhere. In 2011, HDTV had the show, "House Hunters," removed from Roku menus. It is still available on Plex and users can still access episodes of this show.

Add four-digit pin protection

Tip 20 - Protecting your credit card information

There are no parental controls on Roku, so how do you keep children from running up a bill on social media sites and leaving your name on the bill? One of the best ways is having a four-digit code that must be entered before a purchase can be made. This stops teens from grabbing the credit card and making purchases without Mom's permission. This pin only applies to purchases though and users can still access public TV channels and private, free channels that have been downloaded to the Roku. Did you know that there are at least two channels on Roku that offer 'adult entertainment' on Roku machines? While these channels are not listed publicly, they can be accessed publicly. However, children must have the codes to be able to access some of this adult content that is considered 'soft porn.' There are channels such as 'Girls Gone Wild,' that may not be appropriate for younger children. Without parental controls, how can parents keep their children from seeing pornagraphic material or adult entertainment that is not suitable for children under age 16? There may not be parental blocks that parents can install, but parents can use a four-digit pin. By having a four-digit pin, a child would have to know the pin before they could access questionable material. This allows parents to access the adult entertainment using their secret pin, while still keeping their children safe from material that has sexual content.

Control the stream rate

Tip 21 - Control how much information your Roku receives at once

If you are having problems with the picture freezing on your Roku? There may be a easy way to keep your Roku from freezing every few minutes. Roku always tries to find the best streaming rate before beginning a video. However, if you would like to change the streaming rate, this is easily done. If you are using the installed software versions of Roku, you can change the streaming rate by the following code on a Roku remote: Home, home, home, up, up, left, right, left, right, left. If you want to check the quality settings for the picture and change the streaming rates, you can use this code: Home, home, home, home, home, rewind, rewind, rewind, fast forward, fast forward. If you need to reboot your Roku, you can also do so by using the following code: Home, home, home, home, home, up, rewind, rewind, fast forward and fast forward.

Stopping the switch

Tip 22 - Stop Roku from changing your featured theme

If you have downloaded a number of channels, it is easy to organize them into the groups that you want by adding a simply code. To move a channel where you want it, all you have to do is to select it and the press the asterisk key on your Roku remote. A submenu will appear on your television screen. This screen will let you to rearrange the channel position and once the channel icon is selected, you will easily be able to move it anywhere you want. You may want to make certain that the setting that says "Featured Themes" is also checked. This means the Roku will not keep changing themes on users, unless a user makes the theme screen change themselves.

Add your own gaming channel - Twitch

Tip 23 - Increase the number of games you can play on your Roku

One way to do this is to add your own private Roku channel. If you already are a gamer, you may have heard of Twitch. The service was launched in 2011 and has over 35 million users, playing on Rokus across the country. What some people may not know is that the creators of Twitch are the same creators who invented Justin.tv, Justin Kan and Emmett Shear. How can you find a game to play? Here is where you have several options. You can stream and find someone who you like their playthroughs and see what they are playing and add it. If you like a game title, you can search to see if it is available as a live cast that is streaming. This channel must be added as a private channel on your Roku, and this can be done easily by going to the Twitch TV for Roku link. You will need to log into your Roku account in order to add Twitch to your current lineup of private channels.

Save money

Tip 24 - Cut down a Streaming bill when traveling if there isn't unlimited Data

No one wants to pay for more data than they actually use. One way to cut down on the data usage while traveling is to change to SD quality settings on Netflix before you start streaming from your Roku 2 or 3 or HDMI streaming stick. This trick will significantly reduce the size of the data streamed from 4GB on the best default setting, to a mere 600MB, when you use a mobile hotspot, Netflix, and a Roku? This will also save you expensive fees for going over your allotted data usage for the month.

Lost remote

Tip 26 - Stop searching for your Roku remote

If you find yourself searching for your Roku remote every time you want to watch television, there is one way you crafty (and handy) way to keep your Roku remote in one place and end the searches. Glue some small strips of velcro to the back of your Roku remote. Glue some velcro strips to the topside of your TV. This will allow you velcro the strips together and hold your remote on your television when it is not in use. This is a big help for Roku users who do lose their remotes. They will never have to search for their Roku remotes before.

Optimize your Wi-Fi to improve Roku picture quality

Tip 27 - Improve the picture quality and the speed at which Roku streams on Wi-Fi

To check your connection speed and see how fast your Roku is sending information to your TV screen, go to the secret Wi-Fi screen. You can find it by entering the following button sequence while you are at the home screen: Home, home, home, home, home, fast forward, down, rewind arrow and fast forward. You can test your network speed by using Vudu, and you do not have to pay for this app. The network testing available on Vudu will tell you what kind of connection that your Roku is capable of handling given your television setup. Having a good signal for your Roku is dependent on your router, but it also depends on your Internet connection. For the best Roku viewing experience, you really need a 1.5 bpm in order to use Roku. How can you tell if your signal is good? The lower the RSSI numbers and if you have a green signal, your Roku should work well and moving your router closer to your Roku will improve the Wi-Fi quality.

Mix a new Roku with an old router

Trick 28 - Update a Roku and use a newer Roku with an old router

If you bought a newer Roku 3 and want to use it, but you have a router that is at least six years old, don't despair when your Roku doesn't work out of the box. What happens if you get the following error message: Error Code 014. Did you know there is a secret way to upgrade your Roku 3 so that it works with an older router? All you have to do is enter home, home, home, home, home, fast forward, fast forward, fast forward, rewind and rewind on your Roku remote, even if you Roku is not connected to the Internet or not. By entering these buttons on your remote, your Roku will bring up a screen that gives you the option to update software. However it will take upgrading your software to your Roku. In order to disable the ping when you do upgrade your software, you will need to push the following buttons in this sequence on your remote: Home, home, home, home, home, fast forward, play, rewind, play fast forward. This secret code will take you to a platform screen, where you can have the option of disabling the network ping. Once the network ping is disabled, you can finish setting up your Roku 3, with an older router. Once you tell it to disable the network pings, hit "Ok" on your remote and hit the back button to return to the home screen. Unplug and replug back in and repower up your Roku. If it does not work, try unplugging all cords again after following the secret screens to upgrade the Roku and disable network pings.

Protecting your playlist

Tip 30 - Play your music in a cloud

MP3 files and video files can be uploaded to Rokus, so that homeowners can watch their favorite videos or listen to their favorite songs on their Roku devices. All that is needed is to install the MP3tunes.com channel under the music section of the Roku menu. While MP3tune.com does offer two free accounts, users can also get much more space, 50 GB of storage for their files, for $4.95. The best news for those who are Roku users is that they can sign up via Roku and get a free upgrade to their account. Why listen to your favorite lyrics in a cloud? Your music choices may not take up as much storage space on a Roku than if you left the files on your Smartphone.

Debugging your Roku

Trick 31 - Use a secret code to get debugging option on TV screen

From time to time, it may be good to debug your Roku. But, getting to a screen that gives you the option might be difficult to do. This is, until you have the code to debug your Roku by pressing the following buttons on your remote: Home, home, home, home, home, fast forward, fast forward, fast forward, rewind, rewind. How do you know if the code you entered is correct? You should be able to see your wireless Mac address and media access control address for an ethernet port, if your Roku has one. You should also see the Roku channel store server, the serial number and build number of your Roku. It will also show you your IP address, which is usefully if you want to do some tweaking to your IP address and add Roku private channels. Have you ever wondered how long your Roku box has been on without having to be restarted? This secret screen, which gives you debugging options, will also tell you your machine's uptime, or time you machine has gone without a reset or restart.

Wipe a hard drive before sell an old computer

Tip 32 - Easy way to clean your machine for resell

If you were have problems with your machine and simply want to get the latest machine, it is easy do a factory cleaning on your Roku and put it up for sale. It can be useful if you do plan on selling your machine because a factory reset will wipe away everything you have installed, bringing your Roku back to the settings it had when you first took it out of the box. Simply hit these buttons on your remote in this order and click the 'Factory Restore' setting: Home, home, home, home, home, fast forward, fast forward, fast forward, rewind, rewind.

Know the exact versions of your TV channels

Tip 33 - Know what version of TV channels you have on your Roku

Did you know there is a way that you can see what versions of TV channels are on your Roku player? This is helpful because you can find the exact code that you need to install a certain TV channel or private channel. This also includes official Roku channels. There is a trick to accessing the list. Here is the button sequence to get the list: Home, home, home, up, up, left, right, left, right, left. To scroll down the list of available channels and versions, simply hit 'Previous,' 'Next,' and 'Done.'

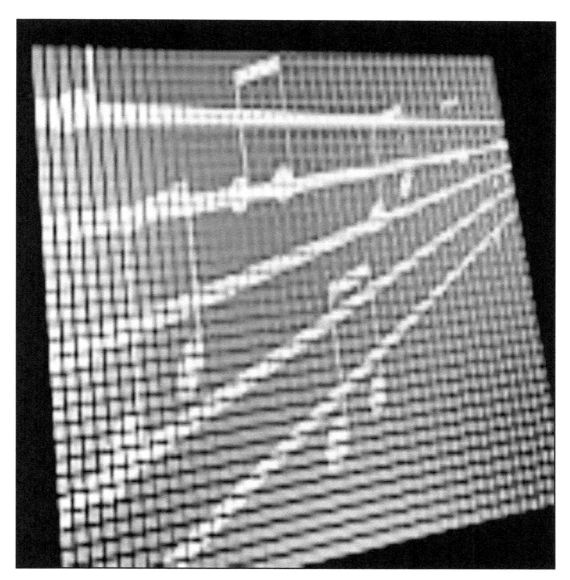

Avoid flashing Roku screensavers

Tip 35 - Don't let fashing screensavers steal your sleep

Is the flashing of a Roku screensaver keeping you awake at night? Did you know there are other options for screensavers that do not have to steal your sleep? The Ouroborealis channel on Roku offers a psychedelic screensaver that is gentler on the eyes and said to promote "zen." Users just need to make sure that they enable their screensaver by going to the setting options in Roku and making sure the box that says 'Enable' is marked.

Find new music on Roku

Tip 36 - Listen to the newest, freshest sounds on Roku

Roku has the SoundCloud Connect channel, which allows Roku users to listen to the newest collaborations made by independent musicians and also famous musicians from around the globe. Did you know that the SoundCloud Connect app will be expanding in the future to include music services such as 8tracks, Jamendo, MixCloud and BandCamp? SoundCloud Connect is free, but some of the other music services may not be. However, Roku users can find what music suits their tastes and also they can fill their library with music from independent and famous musicians' songs. It may be a good way to help insomnia. It also is a good way to save and keep from spending several dollars on an album where customers only like one or two songs.

Block ads on Roku

Trick 37 - Block advertisements on your Roku

Did you know that you can block most advertisements on your Roku by adding a domain block once you access your router settings? If you add doubleclick.net and cloudservices.rok.com to the list of ads to block, this may eliminate a majority of the ads showing up on your Roku screen and also blocks the ads from showing up when you are viewing content from YouTube.com. Once you block these websites, you will need to restart your Roku. This will clear the DNS cache and help keep those ads from allowing you to have a enjoyable viewing experience. However, this trick may not work for all Roku 1 models and the streaming stick models that need MHL ports.

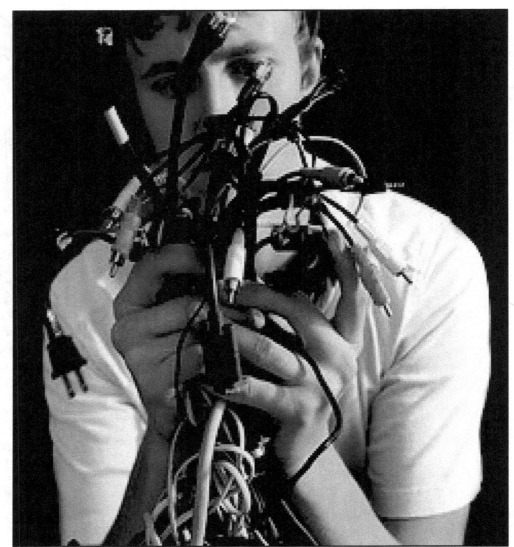

Tie wires turn TVs into 'wireless devices'

Tip 38 - Hide the Roku cords

It is easy to make it seem as though you have a wireless television, by simply picking up the television cords and wires from the floor behind the TV. These cables and cords can be hidden by using one of the plastic ties that are used to keep toys attached to cardboard and can easily be tightened or loosened to accommodate your wiring needs. Cords can be bound together and keep off the floor with these cheap, plastic ties. Not only does it make your living room look nice, but it leaves people wondering whether your television really is a 'Smart TV' that is wireless. Keeping cords up also means that they are not a hazard if you have young children in the house who may trip over the loose cables or try to play with the electrical cords.

Getting the American version of Netflix in foreign countries

Tip 39 - Setup a VPN or Smart DNS to watch Netflix outside Region 1

Whether you are visiting Canada, Germany, Ireland, Denmark or France, it is possible to watch the American version of Netflix channels. However, it may mean you have to set up a VPN or Smart DNS in order to bypass Netflix restrictions. It may also mean having to change your Netflix location if you are using a Roku, Roku 2 or Roku 3. A U.S. account must be created on Roku. You must have an IP address that appears you are living in the U.S. in order to access channels such as: the NBA, MLB, Flixster, Blockbuster on Demand, and many other channels. Having a VPN or Smart DNS allows you to change your IP address to another country and still be able to add Netflix to your Roku account. Roku doesn't openly support having a VPN, so you will need to add one to your router for Roku to use it. Setting up a Virtual Private Network is easy. Check out FreeStream.com, which provides a list of channels that may be added to your machine. Included on this list are VPNs and codes for those networks. Find the code for the network that you wish to add. Go to your Roku account and log on from your home screen. Your Roku will prompt you, asking if you would like to add a channel. Click 'yes' and enter the code for the VPN you wish to add. Do not worry if your VPN does not appear in your list of channels immediately. Twenty-four hours is needed before any added channels will appear on your Roku menu for available channels to watch.

The fun of having a Roku is watching hidden channels on Playon

Tip 40 - Get PlayOn to get access to more content on Roku

PlayOn is a service that allows you to stream programs and then download them to your Roku. While it is not free, it does come with a 14-day free trial and it reasonably-priced at $19.99 a year or $39 for a lifetime. Did you know some programs, such as Hulu offer free service for a computer but, for Roku users, there is no free service? It is only paid, for $8.99 a month. PlayOn acts as a "bridge" and users can get access to 30 different channels. However, content is delivered to a Roku in SD and users must have access to a fairly good computer in order to be successful in using PlayOn.

Limit the bandwidth on the Roku

Tip 41 - Learn to throttle your Roku

It will take all the bandwidth that it can get in some instances. If you have an Internet provider who throttles the information coming through the router, it can also slow down your ability to access your Internet. If you have a data plan and pay for bandwidth usage, there is good cause to cap and throttle how much your Roku uses. To limit your maximum bandwidth, you need to enter the following button sequence code on your Roku remote: Home, home, home, home, home, rewind, rewind, rewind, fast forward, and fast forward. This should bring up a special screen that allows you to change the bandwidth and it also may help to reduce the buffering that your Roku experiences. Setting your Roku to the lowest resolution setting, 480i, may help your Roku run faster and produce better quality overall.

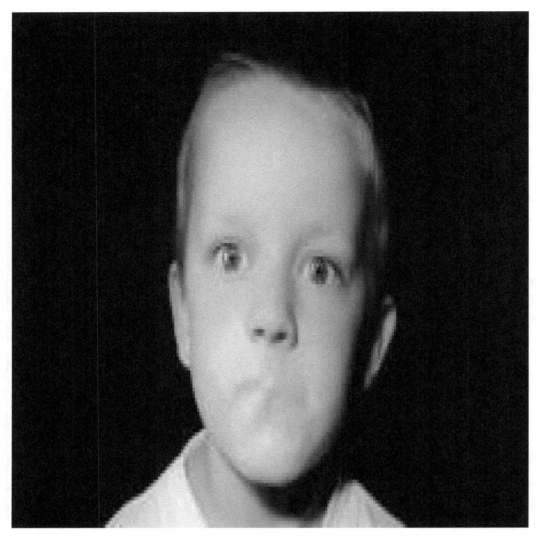

Only for the children

Tip 42 - Have a kids' only Roku

There may be content out on TV that is not good for little eyes to see. By having a "kids-only" Roku box, parents can monitor what their children watch. Adults can approve of the channels that they add to these black boxes before they are added. Parents can feel confident that their children aren't going to have access to questionable adult content, as parents can set their Roku box with a four-digit pin option. This means a four-digit pin must be given before content is downloaded.

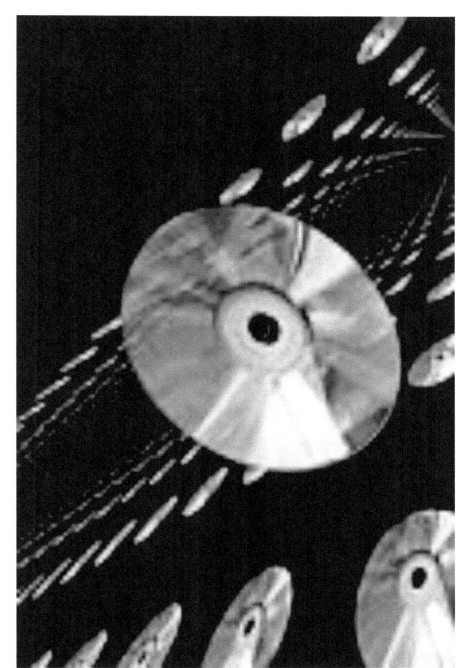
Go digital with DVD copies

Tip 43 - Keep your DVDs from getting scratched by your children

Why not keep digital copies of your favorite DVDs on your Roku? This ensures that your DVD library grows and no DVDs are ever lost because the children scratched them up or the dog decided to chew a DVD. It also allows you to save your space on the bookshelf for books and mementos that are most precious to you. The best part is that you do not have another knick-knack to dust around. Heat or cold will never damage your DVDs.

They can be accessed at any time and if you have a headphone jack on the new Roku 3 devices, a DVD can be watched without disturbing others in the family.

Third parties offer great TV programming

Tip 44 - Try a new channel, KoldCast TV

If you like the layout and interface of Netflix, why not try KoldCast TV? It has the same easy-to-use layout as Netflix and offers users options when it comes to TV content. Since it uses the same navigation tools, it makes sense that KoldCast TV also provides an easy way to receive updates of their content. However, KoldCast TV is only one of many TV channels on Roku. There is also Justin.tv and more. Since there are a number of private television stations, there is also choices when it comes to viewing content. If you don't want to watch the content of one third-party provider, you can always check to see what another provider is offering for free.

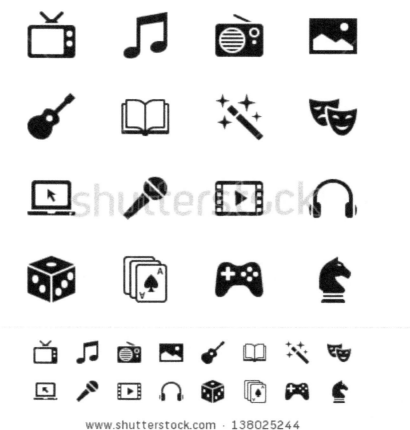

Use Roku's new remote app 3.0 to search

Tip 45 -Search for all movies at the same time

Roku has a remote app that will allow users to search for all movies and TV shows across all Roku channels, not just what is showing in Netflix or Plex. Roku also has their set-top boxes that make it easier for mobile users to navigate and stream. Did you know that this mobile app also has updated text input, so that users can quickly enter private channel codes and other information needed into your Roku box? One thing that has not changed, even with a option to do an universal search is the fact that local content is still supported and can be played back easily. This app may allow more Roku users to watch more movies and content on their boxes, instead of paying a high price to go to a crowded movie theater.

Strengthening your router signal

Tip 46 - Extend your router signal to your Roku

Rokus are amazing machines, but it is hard to enjoy your Roku if it keeps freezing. There are a number of things that may affect your router signal and keep your Roku from being able to stream movies and television channels on your box without frequent pauses. It may be that your routing signal is too far away from your Roku and your streaming device is not getting a strong signal. Problems with a router signal may be because you have an older wireless router and the router may simply need to be upgraded to a newer model. Older routers may not have the capacity to boost your routing signal to the speed needed to comfortably stream. There are programs, such as such as Securifi Almond, that allow users to boost their signal without getting a new wireless router.

Adding channels

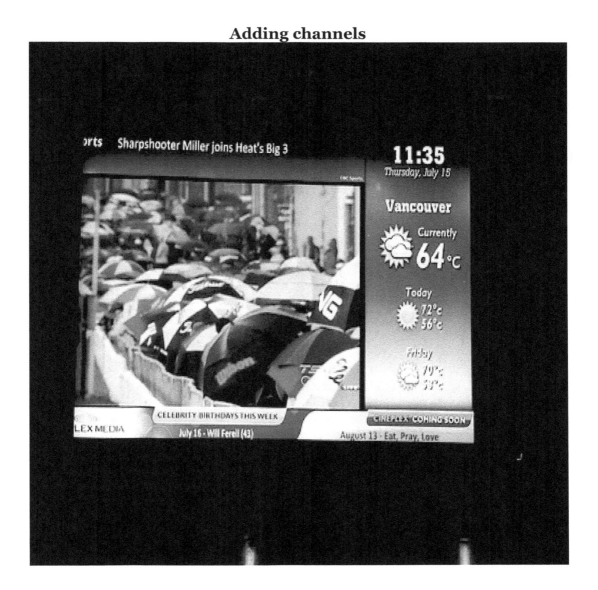

Tip 47 - Increase the channels on your Roku

It is easy to find one of the many channels that are public, private, free or paid at freestreamtv.com. The site also offers reviews on their websites so you can quickly find the best sites. At freestreamTv, Roku users can find codes to add channels that may not necessarily be supported by Roku. However, with more than 1,800 channels that are available for Roku owners. Some of the channels, such as Netflix, do require a monthly fee to access. However, there are channels that allow you find public television stations across the U.S.

Watch PBS most popular show

Tip 48 - Why not catch an episode of 'Downtown Abbey'

This is one of the most popular dramas on PBS. Now in its fifth season, it is hard not to get caught up in the emotional 1920s British drama that has won over American audiences. Based in a time that falls within five years of the Great Depression and in a world where women may talk about politics, this television series brings the drama. It used to be to get this show, users had to enter a code and add the channel manually. There is now an official link to PBS in the Roku home menu, so users only have to click on the PBS link and search for Downtown Abbey.

While Season 5 of the show is airing soon, the cast will be going into production on Season 6 in February. How long does the cast spend filming? It is an intense six months together filming scenes for the show. Though the storyline has progressed 12 years, the cast of this popular TV show stay ever youthful, thanks in part to the magic of cosmetics.

Conclusion

Why buy a Roku? For many it may be the fact streaming public televisions across the United States and subscribing to Netflix is cheaper than buying cable or satellite. Roku offer users a versatile range of options, such as turning your Roku box into a DVR. Roku also offers users the option to hear their favorite musicians, without having to pay for an album or worry about having to have additional equipment, such as an iPod.

For many homeowners with a Roku, it isn't so much the television programs or films that they can watch. It is more about the flexibility of a single machine that allows users to check their phone messages, their email and text, using their television screens and a small, black box. The Roku allows people to stop thinking about their television set as furniture that only has one function. It still may be hard for some to believe that a Roku packs all that power in one, little box that weighs less than three pounds.

Reasons to Buy a Roku

Buying a Roku is not only about saving some money or getting better content than what the cable companies are selling. It also means believing and trusting in the technology. Who ever knew five years previous that anyone would develop the capability to stream content at 4K resolution or that such a small RAM could be placed in such a powerful device. Roku is about joining a future that explores the changing world and allows users to come to their own conclusions and changes, all without charging customers fees to become members, even though Roku owners are already a part of a group and already have a membership. They are members of a company that is redefining what we should and shouldn't be able to do with a simple television set.

Who wouldn't want to belong to a group whose membership wasn't dependent on high monthly fees. If support was offered for Netflix and Amazon Instant, this would be a bonus for owning the newest member of the Roku family. However, the question remains, are we changing the world by having these incredible devices that allow us to operate our TVs as a DVR without having a DVR or are these same devices changing your world and how we interact with those within?

Is technology, such as the Roku driving us to make healthy changes? It may be too soon to tell for the moment. However, one thing is certain. The Roku will not be going away anytime soon. As the technology for the Roku improves, it can only leave us wanting more and more from these little, black boxes. It begs to question, what is next for the Roku after Roku 4? What is the future for these black boxes. Will we see more content streaming from our televisions, or will Roku bring us even something greater in 2016 after everyone has gotten over the shock of having super-fast, streaming service?

www.ingramcontent.com/pod-product-compliance
Lightning Source LLC
LaVergne TN
LVHW060148070326
832902LV00018B/3012